CW01064539

Original title:

Lemur's Leap

Editor: Jessica Elisabeth Luik

Author: Swan Charm

ISBN HARDBACK: 978-9916-86-453-1

ISBN PAPERBACK: 978-9916-86-454-8

Boundless Branches Flight

The sky is wide, with azure might,
Where countless dreams take endless flight,
Upon the wings of hopes so bright,
The boundless branches touch the light.

From roots so deep, the trunk ascends,
Through seasons' turns, it never bends,
In whispered winds, the leaves extend,
And to the sky, their arms they send.

Birds on branches, songs they share,
Their joy and sorrow fill the air,
In chorus, nature's voice declare,
The endless beauty everywhere.

Sunlight gilds the lofty eaves,
Shadowed art by artist leaves,
In time's embrace, the tree still weaves,
A tapestry that never grieves.

Boundless branches, hearts entwined,
With every breeze, their spirits bind,
To sky and earth, their lives aligned,
In boundless flight, pure dreams we find.

Midnight Gymnast

In the hush of silent streets,
A shadow flips and turns with grace.
Stars stand guard, a stellar fleet,
Tracing paths in moonlit space.

Whispers soft in midnight air,
Echo leaps and bounds so high.
Urban jungle, bold and bare,
Lit beneath the starlit sky.

Grace and power intertwine,
Every move, a ghostly trace,
In that witching hour, fine,
Assuming forms the night embrace.

Canopy Dancer

High above the forest floor,
Boughs entwine in leafy waltz.
Whispering leaves, they ask for more,
Of nature's rhythm, no default.

Gliding on the subtle breeze,
Balancing on branches old.
Graceful steps among the trees,
Secrets of the woods unfold.

Sunlight shards through emerald lace,
Nature's ballroom up on high.
Flora's calm and pristine face,
Mesmerized by dancer's nigh.

Serenade of the Silenced

Echoes lost in realms of thought,
Silent melodies unfold.
Unseen singers, lessons taught,
In the quiet, truths are told.

Voiceless tunes the wind conveys,
Waves of sound in gentle sway.
Souls attuned in wordless praise,
Harmony in mute array.

Listen close to whispers deep,
Sonnets plain in silence found.
In the void, emotions seep,
Creating worlds without a sound.

Twilight Tracer

Dusky hues that paint the sky,
Fading light in soft embrace.
Evening's touch, a last goodbye,
Tracing-edge of daylight's grace.

Golden beams through shadows creep,
Drawing lines on twilight's face.
Silent vigil, night does keep,
Softly fades with every trace.

Veil of stars begins to wake,
Skyward journey, gentle chase.
Day departs while night does break,
Leaving stardust in its place.

Balancing Act at Dusk

In the twilight's gentle glow,
Where the fading sun sinks slow,
Shadows stretch, and breezes hush,
Daylight whispers its last blush.

Trees sway in evening's breath,
Dew-kissed leaves unfurl beneath,
Balancing on edge of night,
Softly cradled in moonlight.

Stars awaken, one by one,
Dancing till the night is done,
Night and day converse in shades,
Harmony in dusk parades.

The Night Flyers' Path

As the daylight fades away,
Moths and bats come out to play,
Silent wings within the night,
Chart their course by pale moonlight.

Owl's call in the midnight air,
Leaves rustle, as if to share,
Stories of the darkened hours,
Whispered through the moonlit flowers.

Stars above, like beacons cast,
Guiding on their silent mast,
Night flyers seek their destined path,
In the night's quiet aftermath.

Pinnacles of Curiosity

Mountains stand in silent grace,
Reaching high, they guard their place,
Whispers from the peaks above,
Echo tales of ancient love.

Clouds caress their rugged sides,
Secrets in the mist confides,
Curiosity takes flight,
Scaling heights by day and night.

Paths unworn and trails anew,
Mysteries in every hue,
Pinnacles that touch the sky,
Drawing curious souls to try.

Cloud-Kissed Forest Trails

In the misty morning light,
Whispers greet the waking trail,
Dew upon the leaves so bright,
Nature spins its timeless tale.

Birds accompany the dawn,
Melodies of new day's birth,
Through the trees, a fawn moves on,
Gentle stirrings of the earth.

Sunlight filters through the green,
Patterns dance upon the floor,
Where the ancient woods convene,
Magic reigns forevermore.

Footsteps fall on softened ground,
Breathing in the forest's song,
In this haven, we are found,
Peace that heals, where we belong.

Ascension Among the Vines

Climbing through the verdant maze,
Vines entwine and spirits soar,
In the canopy's embrace,
Hearts are light and troubles pour.

Hands that grasp and feet that tread,
Feel the pulse of life anew,
Leaves above and earth ahead,
Views reveal a sky so blue.

Every step a boundless flight,
Higher still, the soul aligns,
Through the verdure soft and light,
We ascend among the vines.

Echoes of the forest's hymn,
Guide us to the summit's gaze,
Nature's beauty, lush and dim,
In this green and silent praise.

Nocturnal Sylvan Spree

Underneath the starry gleam,
Nymphs and shadows start to play,
In the forest's moonlit dream,
Night becomes a grand ballet.

Whispers of the leaves and trees,
Carry secrets through the air,
Magic fills the twilight breeze,
Midnight's charm is everywhere.

Creatures stir and senses wake,
Paths of silver softly glow,
In the moon's embrace, they take,
Steps where only dreams can go.

Silent echoes of the night,
Weave a spell on all who see,
Mystery in shadows' light,
On this nocturnal sylvan spree.

Grasping at the Moon

Fingers reach to touch the sky,
Hopes aloft on lunar beams,
Dreams ascend, they will not die,
Boundless as the silver streams.

Moonlight drapes the world below,
Bathing all in tender light,
In its glow, our spirits grow,
Wings unfurl in silent flight.

Through the night, our hearts in tune,
With the whispers of the stars,
Yearning hands grasp at the moon,
Seeking out those cosmic bars.

Infinite as night proceeds,
In the dark, our dreams commune,
Lives are stitched with stellar threads,
Always grasping at the moon.

Twilight Treebound Tango

In twilight's gentle, fleeting grace,
The trees begin their nightly dance.
Shadows flicker, intertwine,
In a trance, they lose themselves.

Branches sway with whispered songs,
Leaves waltz through the purple dusk.
Moonlight garlands every limb,
In this twilight treebound tango.

Stars emerge and light the way,
Shimmering above the crest.
Nature's rhythm, caught in sway,
Each verse a lingering caress.

Beckoned by the night's embrace,
A hush that speaks of untold tales.
The twilight treebound tango swirls,
An endless dance, soft and frail.

Beneath the Canopy's Embrace

Beneath the canopy's embrace,
A world unfolds, serene and calm.
Whispers ride the evening breeze,
Nature's hymn, a soothing balm.

Emerald leaves form arcane roofs,
Sheltering souls in restful trust.
In the quietude of dusk,
Their secrets linger, free of rust.

Echoes of the day retreat,
As moonlight weaves a silver lace.
Crickets sing their requiem,
Beneath the canopy's embrace.

Infinite in peace and grace,
The boughs stand sentinel and wise.
Guardians of ancient lore,
Their whispers rise towards the skies.

A Nocturnal Ballet

Underneath the velvet night,
A ballet begins, soft and grand.
Creatures waltz in moon's attempt,
To sketch dreams with shadowed hand.

Fireflies ignite the stage,
Twinkling like the stars above.
Owls with graceful, silent flight,
Join the dance, with muted love.

Rustling leaves compose the score,
Nature's notes in perfect sweep.
In this nocturnal ballet,
Every heart is captured deep.

Cast against the astral cloth,
The dancers move in harmony.
Enchanted by the night's allure,
In this secret symphony.

Arboreal Adventure Awaits

Beneath the arching, leafy spires,
An arboreal adventure starts.
Whispers call from hidden trails,
Inviting brave and curious hearts.

Mossy carpets, emerald bright,
Guide the steps through twilight's veil.
Ancient trunks with stories carved,
Reveal life's subtle, tender tale.

Canopies block daylight's glare,
Weaving shadows, cool and deep.
In the forest's tranquil breath,
Secrets gathered, promises keep.

Venture forth, dear wanderer,
Where nature's beauty never waits.
In every rustling branch and leaf,
An arboreal adventure awaits.

Between Branches' Embrace

Sunlight filters in a gentle trace,
Through the leaves' tender veil,
Nature's song in soft embrace,
Tells an ancient, whispered tale.

Winds weave through the forest green,
Carrying secrets old and wise,
Every rustle, every unseen,
Echoes where silences rise.

Nestled in the branches high,
Creatures find their hidden lairs,
Within the canopy of sky,
Life breathes in wooded prayers.

A symphony of rustling leaves,
Dances on the forest floor,
Where time itself finds reprieve,
And ages past are florid lore.

Whispers in the Wilderness

Voices of the wilderness speak low,
Through the twilight's fading grace,
Mysteries in the wind's soft flow,
Whisper truths of time and space.

Beneath the twilight's deepening hue,
Shadows dance in spectral waltz,
Where the wild things true,
Follow paths in silent vaults.

Footsteps tread on nature's scroll,
Leaving prints in ancient dust,
In the wilderness, the spirit whole,
Finds a kinship free from rust.

Stars above in vigil keep,
Glimpse the secrets earth beholds,
In the wilderness, dreams sleep,
Woven in nature's manifold.

Among Jungle Giants

In the realm where giants sway,
Nature whispers in the dark,
Every root and vine convey,
Life's eternal, vibrant spark.

Emerald canopies stretch wide,
Guardians of an ancient lore,
In their shade, secrets hide,
Tales untold for ages more.

Rivers carve their winding path,
Through the jungle's living maze,
In their flow, no human wrath,
Can disrupt the primal daze.

Birds of countless colors sing,
To the rhythm of the dawn,
Their melodies in echoes ring,
Until the night has gone.

Moonlit Canopy Climbers

Beneath the moon's soft silver light,
Shadows climb the ancient trees,
In the stillness of the night,
Echoes drift on midnight's breeze.

Whispers of the wild converge,
In the canopy so high,
With each branch and silent urge,
Stars adorn the velvet sky.

Creatures of the night awake,
To the call of lunar glow,
In the shadows, mysteries take,
Forms that only dreamers know.

Climbers stretch to touch the stars,
Guided by the moonlit beams,
In the canopy, near and far,
Lives the essence of our dreams.

Moonlit Jungle Quest

Beneath the silver lunar glow,
Whispers form the path we know,
Guiding feet through moss and fern,
In shadows deep, where secrets burn.

Jaguar prowls with silent might,
Emerald eyes in moon's full light,
Echoes of the night bird's call,
Guardians watch the shadows fall.

Far beyond the river's rush,
Mysteries in the midnight hush,
Ancient faces carved in stone,
Lessons of the long unknown.

Stars twinkle through canopy,
A lantern-woven tapestry,
Through verdant halls, our spirits quest,
In moon's embrace, we find our rest.

Furtive Forest Fables

Beneath the ancient oak's embrace,
Tales of old find sacred space,
Whispered winds and rustling leaves,
Weave the sagas moonlight weaves.

Elfin steps on dew-kissed ground,
Soft as shadows, lost, then found,
Fables sung in breeze's flow,
Secrets whispered long ago.

Mossy stones, a cryptic lore,
Stories carved from time's before,
In the quiet, truths unfold,
Silent voices, echoes old.

Midnight's veil, a storyteller,
Sleepless dreamer, night revealer,
Each branch, each root, a timeless verse,
In forest's heart, our tales immerse.

Dawn's First Acrobatics

Sunrise paints the sky with grace,
Morning breathes in amber lace,
Birdsong heralds day's return,
Nature's chorus, bright and stern.

Dewdrops dance on petal's edge,
Balancing on life's fine ledge,
Light into the dark unfurls,
Spinning pearls and radiant swirls.

Squirrels leap from branch to tree,
Boundless in their revelry,
Morning blooms in gentle arcs,
Moments stitched with nature's marks.

In the dawn's first acrobatics,
Harmony through simplest tactics,
Every creature finds its place,
In the dawn's first warming grace.

Through the Banyan Veil

Beneath the lattice of the green,
Stories past and present seen,
Branches twist and shadows play,
Guiding through the twilight gray.

Roots like fingers touch the ground,
In their grip, old secrets found,
Veins of wisdom, lifelines true,
Leading souls with every clue.

Sunlight filters, sifting gold,
Through the silken leaves, untold,
Every step, a whisper's tale,
Through the ancient Banyan veil.

Time is braided, past, and now,
Eternal in the banyan's bough,
Life's great journey, eons sailed,
Through the veil, the spirit hailed.

Elusive Marvel

In the whisper of morning's dew,
With secrets tender on the breeze,
Nature's hand untold, anew,
Painting dreams upon the leaves.

Each petal holds a tale unsaid,
A marvel hidden from the sight,
In dawn's soft light, so gently spread,
A symphony of pure delight.

If you listen, you might hear
The heartbeat of the waking earth,
A song that soothes away your fear,
And fills your soul with silent mirth.

Dusk's Performer

As the twilight takes its bow,
And shadows waltz with day's embrace,
The night prepares its grand show now,
Stars adorn the evening's face.

A symphony of cricket's tune,
With whispering leaves to keep the time,
Under the gaze of the rising moon,
The world spins stories in silent rhyme.

Fireflies light the darkened stage,
Their glow a dance of hidden might,
A performer with timeless age,
Guiding us through the deep of night.

Night's Wanderer

Underneath the silver glow,
Of moonlight's tender, soft caress,
A wanderer in stardust flow,
Embraces night with quiet press.

Footsteps echo, soft and pure,
On paths where dreams reside and play,
In midnight's arms, serene, demure,
A journey through the lost and fey.

The stars, as maps, guide through the night,
Each one a beacon, guiding home,
An endless quilt of twinkling light,
For wanderers who softly roam.

Ethereal Traveler

Wanderer in the twilight hue,
Across the stars, a journey new.
Silent whispers guide your way,
Cosmic paths at end of day.

Nebulae of dreams unfold,
Galaxies with secrets told.
Lightyears drift like fleeting sighs,
In astral realms where magic lies.

Celestial winds your wings embrace,
Through the void, a gentle trace.
Planets spin beneath your gaze,
Lost in time's eternal maze.

Ethereal skies with endless lore,
Radiant worlds, you will explore.
Chasing shadows, light unfurls,
Traveler of the night's deep swirls.

Stars align in whispered call,
Boundless realms where you enthrall.
Infinite, your quest unbound,
In celestial night, your soul is crowned.

Ephemeral Grace

Moments fleeting, whispers fade,
In the dance of days gone by,
Ephemeral, the night parade,
Of stars that wander in the sky.

Grace that slips through fingers' grasp,
Like sand through time's relentless hand,
Yet in its fleeting, lies a clasp,
To memories that gently land.

A touch, a glance, a fleeting heart,
In the space where dreams align,
Ephemeral, we live, depart,
With grace, our spirits intertwine.

Tales of the Treeline

In shadows deep where roots entwine,
Old oaks and pines their tales combine,
Whispers of time in rustling leaves,
Stories of lands and faded eves.

Ancient are the boughs that bend,
Through storms and calms, they never end,
Echoes of the past they hold,
In their rings, the tales unfold.

Woodland paths where secrets lie,
Underneath a twilight sky,
Walkers hear the murmured lore,
Of a world that came before.

Starlit nights where dreams reside,
Treasures in the forest hide,
Listen to the treetops sing,
Tunes of life and everything.

Winds that weave through green and gray,
Carry memories far away,
From the first light to twilight's sign,
These are the tales of the treeline.

Primordial Dance

In ancient woods, where shadows play,
A serpent winds through roots and clay,
Eternal steps, in endless trance,
A whispered tune, the Earth's romance.

Above the ground, as dusk unfolds,
The night calls forth its quiet holds,
With every breeze, the branches sway,
The forest hums of yesterday.

Leaves flutter down, as dancers glide,
On mists that curl and softly hide,
The timeless waltz of life and chance,
The endless, fleeting, primordial dance.

Treetop Hiatus

High above in canopies vast,
Where time itself seems not to pass,
A pause in haste, a moment's rest,
The treetop's heart, a tranquil nest.

Birds converse in soft delight,
Among the leaves in morning light,
Their melodies drift, pure and bright,
A symphony in silent flight.

Here, the world seems far from gray,
In nature's arms, we steal away,
A treetop hiatus, calm and slow,
Where whispered winds begin to flow.

Forest Ballet

Under boughs of emerald green,
A dance unfolds in twilight's sheen,
With rustling leaves and branches bold,
A ballet in the evening's hold.

The deer steps light on mossy floor,
While shadows weave and spirits soar,
A fawn's soft gaze, the moon's embrace,
A delicate, untamed grace.

Each movement pure, each gesture fine,
In twilit woods, where stars align,
A forest ballet, wild and free,
Nature's art in harmony.

Glimpse in the Green

Deep within the forest maze,
Where sunlight stipples through the haze,
A gentle flash, a fleeting scene,
A secret world caught in between.

The fox slips quick through fern and vine,
A glimmer in the forest's spine,
With eyes alert, in twilight's gleam,
A silent glimpse within the green.

Each hidden path, a tale untold,
With whispers of the ages old,
In every shadow, unseen,
A glimpse of life lived in the green.

Silhouette in the Trees

Moonlit shade, a phantom glide,
Through the forest, silent slide.
Branches whisper ancient lore,
Shadows dance on forest floor.

Leaves rustle in evening's breath,
Hints of life from silent depth.
Faint outline in twilight's crease,
Nature's night, a creeping peace.

Owls hoot in echoed call,
Silent footsteps weave through all.
Beneath the boughs in mystic ease,
Dwells the shadow in the trees.

Midnight secrets held in trust,
In wild groves, the spirits must.
Silent ghost in nature's fold,
Ancient stories yet untold.

Darkness fades with dawn's caress,
Silhouette in soft recess.
Daylight claims the forest's guise,
Night's enigma bids goodbyes.

Silent Acrobatics

Underneath the velvet night,
Stars align in spectral light.
Graceful movements softly blend,
Silent acrobat, transcend.

Twilight whispers through the air,
Balances without a care.
Nimble flights in moon's embrace,
Hidden dancer leaves no trace.

Nocturnal ballet in the dark,
Rhythmic steps on nature's ark.
Shadows leap in quiet arcs,
Through the stillness, beauty sparks.

Ephemeral in nightly dance,
Captured in a fleeting glance.
In the silence, magic thrives,
Soulful grace in twilight skies.

Morning glows with dawning hues,
Eclipsing night's subdued muse.
Yet the memory shall last,
Of silent nights and acrobats.

Nature's Acrobat

High above, the treetops sway,
In the breeze of light's soft fray.
Elegant and free, they dart,
Nature's acrobat, pure art.

Through the woods with nimble grace,
Leaping bounds in swift embrace.
Branches bend beneath their feet,
In the dance where wild meets.

Leaves fall in a spiral flight,
As they move through day and night.
Silent twirls in sun and shade,
In this woodland serenade.

Life's trapeze, their stage anew,
Every leap a sight to view.
Harmony in nature's plan,
Acrobat of earth and span.

Morning glow or twilight's hush,
In their steps, we see the rush.
Of life's rhythm, pure and grand,
Nature's acrobat, unplanned.

Dawn's Filigree Flight

Morning breaks with gilded hues,
Nature stirs with morning dews,
Birds take wing in filigree,
Across the sky, wild and free.

Sunlight dances on the stream,
Awakening the world in gleam,
Golden threads in morning's light,
Guide the day from fading night.

Shadows flee as day awakes,
With the dawn, the night forsakes,
Every leaf and blade in sight,
Kissed by dawn's soft, tender light.

Mountains stand in majesty,
Touched with dawn's embroidery,
Silent witnesses of flight,
Of the dawn and her delight.

Glistening with the morn's embrace,
Heaven stitches time and space,
As dawn ascends and takes her place,
In the heart of morning's grace.

Twilight's Hold on the Trees

When the sun's last glow does fade,
In the forest, shadows wade,
Twilight wraps the woods in guise,
Stars appear in azure skies.

Trees in twilight hold their own,
Silent as the night is grown,
Branches whispered, cool and still,
Echoes of the nighttime thrill.

Dusky trails where secrets play,
In the dimming light of day,
Moonlit paths and silent breeze,
Weave their way amidst the trees.

Darkened silhouettes abound,
In the twilight's gentle sound,
Every leaf and twig seems bold,
Under twilight's subtle hold.

Night's embrace so softly spun,
Curfew of the setting sun,
In the forest shadows freeze,
Bound by twilight's hold on trees.

Whispered Secrets of Twilight

In the hush of twilight's fall,
Nature's whispers softly call,
Secrets murmur in the breeze,
Through the leaves and past the trees.

Crickets sing and fireflies gleam,
Under twilight's gentle dream,
Spirits of the night arise,
Dancing 'neath the velvet skies.

Mystic shadows stretch and creep,
In the twilight's downward sweep,
Whispers of forgotten times,
Echo through the silent chimes.

Moonlight filters through the air,
Highlighting the secrets there,
Mysteries in twilights' shroud,
Silent and yet oh, so loud.

Whispered secrets, dusk does weave,
Through the night's soft-spoken sieve,
Twilight's tales to night bequeath,
Guarded by the shadows' sheath.

Through the Canopy's Maze

Sunlight dapples, leaves interlace,
Emerald shadows shift with grace.
Whispers of the ancient trees,
Guide us through with tender ease.

Paths untangle, branches sway,
Serenade of a dim-lit day.
Crickets hum their evening tune,
Guided by the silver moon.

Vines descending, mossy floor,
Nature's tales forevermore.
Echoes of forgotten lore,
We venture forth, our spirits soar.

Roots like veins in twilight's hue,
Skyline peeking, none too few.
Through the maze of green and gold,
Mysteries of the woods unfold.

Heartbeats match the forest's song,
Footprints laid, we do belong.
Silence speaks where words may fail,
Canopy's maze, our secret trail.

Velvet Night Ascension

Stars aligned in endless night,
Bathed in velvet's softest light.
Whispering winds of twilight calm,
Cradle dreams within their palm.

Moon ascends, a silver queen,
Casting shadows, soft serene.
Nighttime blooms in fragrant air,
Cosmic dance beyond compare.

Silent echoes, soft refrain,
Heaven's music, sweet and plain.
Luminous in dark's embrace,
Night ascends with poised grace.

Constellations paint the sky,
Stories etched where spirits fly.
Galaxies in velvet bound,
Celestial whispers, profound.

Mortal hearts and stardust weave,
'Neath the shroud of night we cleave.
In the dark, our souls discern,
Velvet night, our hearts return.

The Secret Forest Ballet

Morning dew and cobweb lace,
Nature's dancers take their place.
Whirling leaves in silent song,
Sunrise brings them, light and strong.

Wisps of fog in golden rays,
Mist-clad ballet, dawn's embrace.
Fawns and fairies, supple grace,
Twirl within their secret space.

Ferns unfold, a verdant stage,
Flora waltzes, age to age.
Creek's soft murmur, pure refrain,
Echoes through the forest's vein.

Birdsong fills the sylvan hall,
Nature's rhythm, rise and fall.
Sunbeams play the leading role,
Casting light on every soul.

In the wood, by daylight's sway,
Continues on the secret ballet.
Witness pure spells softly cast,
Ephemeral, it shall last.

Moon's Captivating Carousel

Gilded moonlight, soft and clear,
Turns the night in rhythmic cheer.
Stars in chorus, chiming bright,
Join the carousel of night.

Orbs of silver, circles wide,
Dance in heavens, side by side.
Whispers in the midnight air,
Moon's embrace, a lover's fare.

Spinning tales of yesteryears,
Lunar glow allays our fears.
Dreams aloft on moonbeam trails,
Nighttime's wondrous, silken sails.

Shadows shift in gentle light,
Silver path through velvet night.
Mystic turns with cosmic zeal,
Eternal, this celestial wheel.

Hearts aglow in moon's soft spell,
Ride the night's great carousel.
Bound by stars, we find our way,
Til dawn sings a new ballet.

Mystic Balancer

On threads of fate, she gently strides,
Between the worlds, her secret hides.
A dance of shadows, light entwined,
In realms of dreams, her power finds.

With whispers soft, she casts her spell,
In twilight's glow, where spirits dwell.
The stars align, her path reveals,
A truth unspoken, time conceals.

Celestial guide, through night she soars,
In silence kept, where wisdom wars.
A calm embrace, the world renews,
In balanced steps, her heart pursues.

Through veils unseen, her presence feels,
The hidden truths the dark unseals.
Her gentle hand, a touch of grace,
In cosmic dance, finds her place.

Whispering Watcher

In forests deep, where shadows play,
The whispering watcher starts her day.
With silent grace, her eyes perceive,
The stories told by rustling leaves.

A guardian of the twilight veils,
In every breeze, she hears the tales.
The secrets of the ancient trees,
Are whispered softly by the breeze.

With every dawn, her vigil keeps,
Beneath the stars, where silence seeps.
Her presence known to those who see,
The watcher in the forest free.

In hallowed woods, her legend grows,
The whispering watcher, nature knows.
A silent force in shadows cast,
Her wisdom ancient, shadows past.

Through Madagascar's Greens

In lush expanse, where colors gleam,
Through Madagascar's vibrant dream.
The canopy, a living veil,
Hides secrets in its emerald trail.

With lemurs' dance and chameleons' glance,
A tapestry of life's romance.
In every branch, a tale unfolds,
In verdant depths, where time beholds.

The river's song, the jungle's breath,
In harmony, a dance of death.
Yet life renews in constant sway,
Through Madagascar's green array.

The baobabs that tower high,
Against the canvas of the sky.
A living land, where magic weaves,
Through every vine, among the leaves.

Whiskers in the Canopy

On branches high, where sunlight beams,
The feline's grace fulfills her dreams.
With whiskers keen on jungle scenes,
She prowls the world amidst the greens.

A shadow swift in canopy's sweep,
Through twilight fades, her secrets keep.
In whispers soft, the forest speaks,
Of whiskers brushed against the peaks.

Her silent steps, a hunter's guise,
In leaves concealed from prying eyes.
A force of nature, fierce and free,
The heart of this wild symphony.

Through night and day, she charts her course,
In twilight's realm, her silent force.
A whispered tale, her legacy,
The whiskered one, crowned canopy.

Clandestine Dancer

Beneath the twilight's veiled embrace,
A figure moves with silent grace,
In moonlit realms, they softly prance,
A secret, hidden, mystic dance.

The shadows play upon the ground,
With whispered steps that make no sound,
A waltz that none are meant to see,
A midnight's covert revelry.

Stars above, in hushed delight,
Gaze upon this spectral sight,
Their twinkling eyes, they never glance,
Away from this forbidden dance.

The winds join in with gentle sighs,
As feet drift past with deft disguise,
Each movement, pure, a cryptic trance,
Of the clandestine dancer's chance.

But as dawn threatens night's pure veil,
The dancer fades, a fleeting tale,
Leaving behind a trace, so faint,
Of what the night and dark conflate.

Forest Nightfall

As daylight wanes in crimson hues,
The woodland whispers ancient news,
Of creatures cloaked in twilight's scrawl,
That wake beneath the nightfall's thrall.

Branches weave a shaded crown,
Where shadows slip and settle down,
The forest breathes a quiet sigh,
As stars ignite the inky sky.

With velvet paws on mossy bed,
Foxes tread where moonlight's shed,
Owls hoot out their hollow song,
To echo where the dark belongs.

Leaves rustle with a mystic hum,
To nature's soft and timeless drum,
Bathed in silver, night's embrace,
Transforms the woods, an ethereal place.

In this serene, enchanted night,
Dreams take flight in whispered light,
Forest nightfall's tender call,
Enfolds the world in its thrall.

Glimmer of Shadows

Where light and dark begin to blend,
A dance of shadows, never end,
They flicker in the candle's breath,
A silent pact with creeping death.

They clothe the walls in mystic form,
Each shift a moment, softly born,
In corners, alcoves, hidden nooks,
Their presence writ in ghostly books.

Moonbeams pierce the night's thick veil,
Drawing out the shadows' trail,
A glimmer here, a shimmer there,
A spectral show beyond compare.

In darkened glass, reflections tease,
The eye that seeks and mind that sees,
But shadows guard their ageless lore,
A silent riddle to implore.

Beneath the stars, in night's cocoon,
They weave the dusk with silent rune,
Glimmering in their silent cries,
The shadowed night ever implies.

Canopy Serenade

In the heart of the verdant boughs,
A symphony in whispers vows,
To sing beneath the emerald shade,
A timeless, tender serenade.

Birds compose with feathered quill,
A melody that won't stand still,
Their notes embrace the leafy heights,
And dance among the sun's warm lights.

The wind becomes a gentle tune,
Humming soft beneath the moon,
It sways the branches, leaves, and more,
A lullaby, the forest's core.

The insects chirp in rhythmic song,
A chorus where the small belong,
Together, in this sacred glade,
They craft the canopy serenade.

As twilight spills its colors wide,
The songs persist, in peace abide,
A symphony that will not fade,
Eternal canopy serenade.

Moonlit Treetop Serenade

Beneath the moonlit sky,
The treetops gently sway,
A serenade, so soft,
Unfolds the night in play.

Whispers in the leaves,
A rustling lullaby,
Stars above will grieve,
For the dreams that say goodbye.

Owls hoot in chorus,
Cicadas join the tune,
Together they adorn us,
In this tranquil night's cocoon.

Echoes of the twilight,
Resonate through air,
Guided by the soft light,
We find solace there.

The forest breathes in time,
With nature's gentle thrum,
A moonlit, hushed rhyme,
Where all our worries numb.

Dancing Through the Vines

In tangled vines, we weave,
A dance of pure delight,
Steps that twist and interleave,
Guided by moonlight.

Whispers from the foliage,
A symphony of green,
To nature, homage,
In this enchanted scene.

Our movements, light as air,
Silent forest applauds,
Mystical, yet rare,
Amongst nature's gods.

Vines cradle and entwine,
A dance of ancient lore,
In shadows, stars align,
Binding forevermore.

Barefoot on the soil,
Through whispers of the pine,
We dance, hearts uncoil,
Lost in rhythm divine.

Shadowed Jungle Paths

Through paths where shadows fall,
The jungle calls our name,
Mysteries in the sprawl,
An eternal, untamed game.

Footsteps soft as whispers,
Leaves crunch with each stride,
In the darkness, slivers,
Where secrets like to hide.

Creatures of the dusk,
In shadows, come to play,
Amidst the scent of musk,
Night replaces day.

Moonlight flickers, lost,
In canopy's embrace,
Guided despite cost,
Through nature's hidden face.

Wanderers of night path,
In twilight's gentle grip,
Sharing nature's breath,
On this shadowed trip.

Whispered Secrets of the Forest

In the quietness, we hear,
Secrets shared by trees,
Whispers oh so near,
Carried on the breeze.

Mysteries untold,
In the rustling leaves,
Stories from the old,
Only heart believes.

Glimpses of the past,
Through bark and bough revealed,
In the forest's cast,
Where truths are unconcealed.

Branch and root, they speak,
Of times that came before,
In their language, weak,
We unravel more.

Night enfolds their tales,
In a symphony profound,
The secrets in the veils,
Of the forest's sacred ground.

Eyes in the Twilight

As dusk drapes the sky in purple hues,
Stars begin their nightly ballet,
An owl's gaze pierces the dark blues,
Guiding night through its silent array.

Luminous orbs watch over the land,
Silent sentinels of the moon,
In twilight's arms, where shadows expand,
Mysteries whisper their tune.

Eyes in the twilight, guardians brave,
Embrace the secrets night has found,
Between the starlight and the wave,
Truths of the cosmos slowly unbound.

Whispers of dusk weave through the air,
Enigma cloaked in twilight's guise,
With every glance, you feel the stare,
Eyes in the dark, wise and wise.

In the quiet, the world reveals,
Stories etched in the night's deep well,
Eyes in the twilight, imprint and seal,
Tales that in silence dwell.

Graceful Climbers' Waltz

Vines entwine in a delicate dance,
Reaching skyward, step by step,
Earth's adornment takes its stance,
In nature's ballet, they adept.

Leaves pirouette on whispered sighs,
Tracing paths in summer's breeze,
Elegance found where beauty lies,
Amongst the branches, swaying ease.

Graceful climbers waltz in green,
A concert of life and motion,
Softly treading, unseen queen,
In the garden's vast devotion.

Flowers bloom as partners sway,
Harmonious in their ascent,
To the melody of day,
Each movement, a life well-spent.

In the realm of moss and wood,
This waltz unfurls, unbidden,
With every climb, misunderstood,
Nature's truth, softly hidden.

Scent of the Wild Hibiscus

A breeze carries whispers of bloom,
Petals crimson, pure delight,
Filling the air with its perfume,
Hibiscus wild in the light.

Morning sun and dew embrace,
Kissing leaves in sweet breeze stride,
Scent of the wild, a timeless place,
Memory forever to bide.

In gardens lush or paths untouched,
Its fragrance, an unseen thread,
Tie us to earth and stars so much,
Deep roots where footsteps tread.

Hues that speak of tropic dreams,
Swaying gently in day's caress,
Perfume woven in sunbeams,
Simplicity in its dress.

Hibiscus wild, heart unfurled,
Scent that carries soul on air,
In garden realms of this world,
Beauty's essence, pure and rare.

Whispers Among the Leaves

In the quiet of the grove,
Leaves converse in gentle songs,
Each whisper a tale of love,
Nature's poetry belongs.

Breezes translate secret words,
Rustling branches in reply,
Symphony of unseen birds,
Echoes through the canopy high.

Sunlight filters soft and warm,
Through the foliage green and bright,
Whispers weave in subtle form,
Blessing the day with soft light.

Each rustle a story's claim,
History in verdant script,
In every murmur, hear the name,
Of ancients whose roots dipped.

Magic in the air they weave,
In the realm of shaded eaves,
Listen close to what they leave,
Whispers among the leaves.

Aerial Prowess

High above, the heavens call,
Wings spread wide, I feel so small,
Clouds like dreams beneath me fall,
In endless skies, I lose it all.

The sun's warm breath upon my face,
I navigate this boundless space,
A bird's domain, a fierce embrace,
In silent whispers, I find my place.

Glimpses of the world below,
A patchwork quilt in sunlight's glow,
From such great heights, the rivers flow,
In flight, I let my spirit grow.

Stars will guide in twilight's wane,
Night unfolds its darkened reign,
Through moonlit lanes, I'll soar again,
In boundless flight, my heart's domain.

Mystery in Motion

Shadows dance in twilight's keep,
Silent figures, secrets deep,
With every step, a promise they speak,
In velvety night, through dreams they creep.

Fleeting moments, doubts unwind,
Whispers echo in the mind,
Chasing whispers, realms confined,
In lurking shadows, truth we'll find.

Through mist and fog, their path undrawn,
Mystery's veil, in silence dawn,
An enigma, forever gone,
In veiled dance, the world is worn.

Unseen forces play their game,
Life and dream without a name,
In their motion, all the same,
Lost in shadows, unseen flame.

Jungle's Ghost

Silent steps on verdant floor,
In shadows thick, spirits soar,
Among the trees, where wild things roar,
In nature's grip, our hearts explore.

Ancient secrets trees disclose,
Where giant roots and rivers flow,
The jungle's breath, a calming blow,
In hidden realms, we come to know.

Faint whispers in the leaves do wake,
Echoes of the past they make,
Nature's call we must intake,
In green embrace, fears will break.

Specter of the wild unseen,
In every branch and every sheen,
The jungle's ghost, forever keen,
In its depths, our souls do glean.

Veiled Navigator

In the twilight, stars will rise,
Guiding hearts in darkened skies,
A navigator, wise and wise,
With veiled eyes, the night complies.

Through cosmic seas, the course is set,
Paths unknown, with no regret,
In stellar maps, we're not misplaced,
Each constellation kindly met.

Moonlit tides, they ebb and flow,
Secrets whispered, winds that blow,
Our guide through night's uncertain show,
In silent trust, we come to know.

Beneath the shroud, with faith-filled stride,
The universe as friend and guide,
O' veiled navigator, we confide,
In you, we let our dreams reside.

Moonlit Balancer

On tightrope spun of silver strands,
She dances in the night,
With grace that only moonlight grants,
She shimmers soft and bright.

Above the world, she weaves her tale,
In sky so deep and hue,
A ballerina pale and frail,
Yet constant, firm, and true.

A step, a twirl, a silent dream,
Her movements light as air,
In moonlit glow, her spirits beam,
A picture pure and rare.

The stars, her audience in flight,
They watch with silent gaze,
As she commands the canvas night,
A mistress of delays.

Her dance a night-thread, bold and neat,
In galaxy confined,
A timeless trek of nimble feet,
A balance redefined.

Treetop Acrobat

High in the canopy's embrace,
Where sunlight rarely sees,
An acrobat with nimble grace,
Swings through the mystic trees.

His limbs, a blur of endless flare,
With leaps from branch to branch,
A master of the fragile air,
In daring, close-knit dance.

The treetops bend to his deft will,
Each leap a venture wild,
With every jump, the forest still,
Enthralled by Nature's child.

Through dappled shade and whispering leaves,
He carves a path unknown,
A journey only he perceives,
Among the vast, alone.

In twilight's deep, he finds his rest,
Beneath the emerald dome,
The treetop acrobat is blessed,
With forest as his home.

Whispering Forest Eyes

In forest deep, where shadows lie,
Amid the ancient boughs,
The trees with whispering eyes do spy,
With solemn, sacred vows.

They watch the world with silent care,
These guardians of green,
Their gaze both wise and unaware,
Of all that's lived and seen.

Through years of sun and winters cold,
Their stories softly told,
With roots that grasp the earth and hold,
Their spirits strong and bold.

Each rustling leaf, a secret shares,
Of earth and sky and man,
A symphony without fanfares,
Played on nature's span.

So walk ye softly, gently tread,
Amid these ancient spies,
And heed the wisdom softly bred,
Beneath their watchful eyes.

Secretive Sprinter

Through the forests deep and dark,
A shadow quickly flees.
Unseen by eyes, unmarked,
It dances with the trees.

Silent as the whispering wind,
It glides on feet like feathers.
No twig or leaf can it rescind,
Escaping all life's tethers.

With grace, it shifts from stone to stone,
A phantom in the night.
Its path remains unknown, alone,
A secret out of sight.

In moonlit glows, it finds its way,
A sprinter in the night.
No chains can lead this heart astray,
It vanishes from light.

In every quiet breath it takes,
A silence fills the air.
The secretive sprinter never wakes,
To let us know it's there.

Nocturnal Navigator

When day gives way to velvet night,
A wanderer takes flight,
His eyes are keen, his heart is light,
He knows the stars by sight.

The woods his map, the sky his guide,
Through paths by moonlight trimmed,
With whispering winds, he strides beside,
Each shadow softly skimmed.

An owl's call, a beacon clear,
To mark his chartless drift,
In realms where midnight creatures peer,
He moves with nature's thrift.

No compass in his hand he needs,
Nor lantern's feeble spark,
For he deciphers whispered creeds,
In shades of deep and dark.

Thus, nocturnal navigator bold,
Through midnight's maze he goes,
A tale of moonlit paths retold,
In nightly, soft repose.

Heights of Hidden Realms

In secret spaces far and wide,
Where whispered winds and shadows glide,
Beyond the mortal, seen by few,
Lie realms of gold and twilight hue.

Peaks that pierce the sapphire skies,
Where ancient voices softly rise,
A world unseen to prying eyes,
Where time eternally defies.

In mystical terrains they bound,
Where only dreams have ever found,
A dance of myths forever sealed,
In heights of hidden realms revealed.

The air with magic subtly teems,
In realms that feed the nightly dreams,
Where moonlight weaves through distant beams,
And silence keeps the sacred seams.

So venture not with heavy heart,
For inner eyes must take their part,
To witness realms of art and light,
In unseen places, out of sight.

In Moon's Gentle Glow

Beneath the canopy of night,
Where silver whispers bathe in light,
The moon in tranquil silence stirs,
And gently soothes the world with lures.

The stars a symphony in dark,
Each twinkle lighting heaven's arc,
A lover's song, a poet's theme,
In moonlit glow, they softly gleam.

Moon's shadowed smile on open sea,
Reflects a calm serenity,
As waves in rhythmic lullaby,
To night's embrace they silently comply.

A gentle hush from nature's breath,
In moon's embrace, there's life, not death,
A moment's pause, a gentle sigh,
Beneath her watchful, velvet sky.

In moon's soft glow, let worries cease,
And drift into the realms of peace,
For night, in secrets, will bestow,
A haven in its gentle glow.

Arboreal Ballet at Dawn

In morning's light, the forest wakes,
With whispered songs the silence breaks,
A dance of branches 'gainst the sky,
As dawn's first breath begins to sigh.

Leaves in soft pirouettes they spin,
With dewdrops glistening on their skin,
An arboreal ballet starts,
Communing with the woodland hearts.

Each bough a limb, they gracefully,
Perform a dance that's wild and free,
A dance with sun's ascending rays,
In harmony with night's relays.

Birds sing their overture so sweet,
In melodies where day and night meet,
With wings of light they join the dance,
In nature's choreographic trance.

Thus dawn bestows its quiet awe,
In nature's grand and gentle law,
An arboreal ballet, profound,
In peace where silent whispers sound.

Through Forest Veils

Between the trees where shadows creep,
Through forest veils, the secrets seep,
A sentinel of ancient lore,
In verdant depths forevermore.

Where mossy carpets softly cling,
And whispers of the wild things sing,
The forest holds its stories tight,
Unveiling only in the night.

In twilight's glow and morning dew,
Through veils of green, the sights are few,
A world untouched by time's cruel hand,
In forest depths, the myths still stand.

Each branch and leaf a woven page,
In tales that span from age to age,
Through shaded paths the journey leads,
Where woodland spirits plant their seeds.

So tread with care, oh wanderer brave,
Through forest veils where legends pave,
For in the whispering trees you'll find,
The echoes of the ancient mind.

Highland Drifter

Upon the peaks where eagles soar,
A soul with nowhere bound.
The winds beneath its feet, they roar,
A nomad on the ground.

Boundless, timeless, without care,
It wanders through the mist.
A drifter to the mountain air,
By nature's hand it's kissed.

Valleys, cliffs, and rugged stones,
Its paths weave through the heights.
In solitude, it walks alone,
Through days and sleepless nights.

The stars become its blanket bright,
The moon its guiding friend.
In twilight's calm and morning light,
Its journeys never end.

Forever shall it roam the high,
A pilgrim of the breeze.
The highland drifter, wild and shy,
At peace with mysteries.

Mysterious Aerialist

Above the world, a figure glides,
Through clouds and open sky.
With every turn, it boldly rides,
Where earthly bounds defy.

A dance against the twilight hue,
A silhouette in flight.
The heavens hold its secret true,
Enfolding in the light.

In crescent moons, it finds its stage,
A performer without peer.
Each motion fluid, free of age,
It lives devoid of fear.

The air becomes its canvas wide,
Each movement like a song.
The rhythmic pulse, the gentle glide,
Where shadows rights the wrong.

In every loop, a whisper heard,
A tale without a voice.
The mysterious aerialist,
In freedom makes its choice.

Ghosts of the Canopy

High above the jungle ground,
In leafy shadows deep.
A presence without sight or sound,
In silence, secrets keep.

They float through branches, scarcely seen,
Specters of the leaves.
In emerald shades and silver sheen,
The forest's breath it weaves.

At twilight's edge, they come to play,
A wisp of spirits past.
Among the boughs, they gently sway,
In dances meant to last.

The moonlight casts their spectral forms,
On treetops lush and high.
Through midnight mists and sudden storms,
They reach toward the sky.

Eternal in their quiet roam,
In canopy's embrace.
These ghosts call the forest home,
In nature's serene grace.

Beneath the Banyan's Laughter

Beneath the banyan's laughter, roots intertwine,
Whispers of old stories, in the wind's soft line.
Leaves that hold the secrets of days gone by,
Branches reach for dreams in the sky.

Dappled light dances on the forest floor,
Where tales are spun and legends soar.
Echoes of laughter, gentle and serene,
In this sacred bower, life feels so keen.

Time moves slowly under its shade,
Memories linger, never to fade.
Ancient and wise, it watches us grow,
Holding the knowledge we yearn to know.

Under its canopy, we find sighs so dear,
Murmurs of the past we're destined to hear.
A sanctuary where hearts find peace,
Beneath the banyan, worries cease.

Ascend the Silent Shadows

Ascend the silent shadows of the twilight's veil,
Ethereal whispers in the night prevail.
Mountains tall stand in mystic haze,
Guiding the lost through twilight's maze.

Silent footsteps echo on paths untread,
Ghostly memories of words unsaid.
Stars gleam faint in heaven's broad hall,
As dreams ascend where shadows fall.

Silent sentinels in the starry hush,
Guarding the stillness, breaking the rush.
Embracing the calm that darkness brings,
In the night's embrace, the soul sings.

Wanderers in the night's embrace,
Find solace in the stars' gentle face.
Ascend the silent shadows we must,
In the quiet, we place our trust.

Between Moonlight and Leaves

Between moonlight and leaves, shadows play,
A dance of night that holds the sway.
Soft whispers of a mystic tune,
Beneath the gaze of a silvery moon.

Crickets sing songs of ancient nights,
Bathed in the cool of lunar lights.
Leaves rustle in a ghostly breeze,
Carrying dreams between the trees.

Caressed by the light, the forest sighs,
A lullaby for stars in the skies.
In this tender dance of the night's fair gleam,
The world succumbs to a serene dream.

Dew-kissed leaves in silence thrill,
With whispered secrets they softly fill.
In a grove where moonlight weaves,
Magic lies between moonlight and leaves.

Orchard of the Night

In the orchard of the night, stars are fruit,
Hanging in darkness, oh so absolute.
Branches of dreams spread far and wide,
Casting shadows where murmurs hide.

Moonbeams filter through the leafy dense,
Touching worlds beyond our sense.
Nocturnal blooms with petals of light,
Blossom gently in the night.

Silent guardians of the twilight hour,
Embrace the calm and unfold their power.
Whispers of wind weave through the night,
Breathing life to shadows, soft and light.

Under this canopy of celestial glow,
Worlds unseen start to show.
In the orchard of the night we find,
Peace eternal for heart and mind.

Twilight's Arboreal Adventure

In the hush of evening bloom,
Forests shiver in twilight's loom,
Leaves whisper tales of skies,
Beneath the fading light, they rise.

Shadows bend to nature's hand,
Luminescent, they take their stand,
Stars peek through the canopy,
Night's adventure, wild and free.

Crickets sing their evening song,
Branches sway, inviting throng,
Mystic paths in moonlit hue,
Guiding souls both old and new.

Owl's gaze cuts through the dark,
Piercing silence with its hark,
In this dance of night's embrace,
Nature reveals its hidden grace.

Whispers of the ancient wood,
Echoes of where giants stood,
Twilight's veil, a curtain thin,
Where each adventure shall begin.

Climbers of the Crescent Moon

Under the watchful lunar light,
Spirits climb to greater height,
Mountains kiss the sky so near,
Crescent moon, their path is clear.

Rocky spires and icy breath,
Challenging the edge of death,
Steps on stone, a sacred tune,
Dancing with the crescent moon.

Whispers on the frost-kissed air,
Legends born of wild dare,
Echoes of the climbers' tale,
In twilight's grip, they prevail.

Stars align as guides above,
Beacons glowing with their love,
Each ascent, a prayer in stone,
To the crescent moon alone.

Valiantly they press and strive,
Their spirits bold, their dreams alive,
Journey on till night is new,
Beneath the moon's soft silver dew.

Sylvan Whispers' Journey

In the grove where secrets lie,
Whispers drift beneath the sky,
Echoes of an ancient song,
Where earth and heaven belong.

Roots entwined in tales of yore,
Silent steps on forest floor,
Listening to the sylvan breath,
Journeying through life and death.

Canopies of verdant veil,
Hide the paths where dreams prevail,
Listening close, you'll hear the call,
Mysteries that bind us all.

River's murmur, brook's soft croon,
Harmonize with nature's tune,
Each leaf tells a storied past,
In whispers' journey wide and vast.

Underneath the time-worn bough,
Future's tender seeds we plow,
Guided by the sylvan voice,
Journeys in the heart rejoice.

Treetop Tango at Dusk

When the sky is painted gold,
Forest fables are retold,
Treetops sway, a dance begun,
Waltzing with the setting sun.

Birds in flight, a rhythmic grace,
In the twilight's soft embrace,
Branches hum a gentle tune,
A tangled tango 'neath the moon.

Squirrels leap from limb to limb,
In the dusky light so dim,
Every step and every twirl,
Part of nature's lively whirl.

Leaves in twilight's gentle breeze,
Whisper secrets to the trees,
Harmonies both bold and shy,
To the twilight's lullaby.

As night descends in velvet sweep,
Forest creatures slowly creep,
Resting in the afterglow,
Where treetop tangos ebb and flow.

Night Climbers' Crescendo

Underneath the moon's embrace,
They scale the heights with silent grace,
Each star applauds their bold ascent,
A dance where night and sky have met.

Whispers of the night wind pass,
Through leaves that shimmer like fine glass,
Their shadows waltz on star-lit stage,
In timeless rhythm, age to age.

Each branch and bough, a daring leap,
To climb the heights where secrets sleep,
Their echoes in the stillness heard,
A symphony without a word.

Above the world, in silent flight,
They journey through the velvet night,
A ballet on the moonlit crest,
Their hearts aloft in quest of rest.

The stars their silent audience,
Bestow upon them reverence,
In darkness they continue on,
Till night surrenders to the dawn.

Woodland Acrobat's Ascent

In the forest's hushed domain,
Through verdant realms where shadows reign,
An acrobat begins to climb,
Embraced by ancient, towering pine.

With nimble paws and tireless grace,
They vanish without leaving trace,
Above the moss, beneath the sky,
They reach for heights where spirits fly.

Their journeys weave through twisted vines,
Exploring realms where magic shines,
Each branch a bridge, each leaf a shield,
Adventure in each bough revealed.

Above the fern and forest floor,
They seek what none have sought before,
A woodland dance on nature's stage,
A timeless saga, page by page.

Through canopies and realms unseen,
Where earth and sky in twilight lean,
They write their tale with each ascent,
In whispers of the firmament.

Secrets of the Silken Sky

Beneath the sky of woven silk,
Where dreams are spun as soft as milk,
The night reveals its hidden lore,
In shadows faint, forevermore.

The stars, like whispers, gently gleam,
In secrets shared from dream to dream,
With luminescence pearls they tell,
Of silent night and twilight spell.

Through constellations, ancient roads,
Where cosmic mystery unfolds,
Their tales entwine in endless sweep,
As worlds within the night do sleep.

Above the earth in vast expanse,
The silken sky begins its dance,
A tapestry of light and shade,
In which the universe is made.

The secrets linger, soft and shy,
In every fold of silken sky,
A quiet hymn of time untold,
In night's embrace, both new and old.

Tangled in Twilight

In twilight's amethyst embrace,
Where day and night in beauty trace,
The tangled webs of dusk advance,
And shadows weave their quiet dance.

The evening star begins to glow,
As twilight winds begin to blow,
Their whispers through the branches passed,
In lullabies that nature casts.

Amidst the hues of purple haze,
Where light and dark in silence gaze,
The woven threads of twilight's lore,
Entwined within the forest floor.

Each silhouette a fading line,
Against the sky where dreams align,
The world in quietude does lay,
As night unfolds the end of day.

In tangled twilight, peace is found,
As dusk and night the earth surround,
A gentle shift from gold to gray,
Till dawn recalls the break of day.

Furtive Forest Fables

In whispered winds, the stories pass,
Through ancient oaks and fields of grass,
Secrets held by roots so deep,
In shadows where the dreams do keep.

The fern and moss, the silent guards,
Hear tales of myths, of ancient bards,
Whispered through the twilight glade,
By moonlit beams, the scenes are laid.

Furtive glances, creatures peek,
From beneath the crust, the earth does speak,
Echoes of the past unwind,
In the forest's heart, the tales are blind.

Each leaf a page, in books of green,
Mysteries by none yet seen,
Timeless words on bark inscribed,
By nature's hand, eternally prescribed.

In the night, the forest breathes,
With voices in the rustling leaves,
The fables float on zephyr's flight,
Through endless days and starry nights.

Nocturnal Woodland Waltz

Stars alight in velvet skies,
Moonbeams cast where silence lies,
A dance begins beneath the hue,
Of twilight's kiss, the night anew.

In rhythmic steps, the shadows play,
Amongst the trees, they softly sway,
The forest, in a gentle trance,
Sways to night's nocturnal dance.

Owls hoot in cryptic rhyme,
In cadence with the flowing time,
The woodland floor, a stage so wide,
Where dreams and whispers closely hide.

Foxes dart in pirouettes,
Through a maze of brambled nets,
Silent paws on mossy glade,
Partake in night's serene parade.

Cicadas sing their lullaby,
Beneath the arc of starlit sky,
The forest, wrapped in twilight's shawl,
Revels in the nocturnal ball.

Jungle's Silent Symphony

Beneath the canopy so wide,
Where verdant layers softly hide,
A symphony of whispers dwells,
In sunless depths, in shadowed wells.

The layers hum with life's embrace,
In every leaf, in every place,
The vines, the branches intertwine,
In melodies both soft and fine.

In silence, yet with voices clear,
The jungle sings for those who hear,
The rustle of the emerald wings,
And songs the silent thicket brings.

Insects hum in gentle chords,
Across the air in tuneful hoards,
Each creature plays a hidden part,
In nature's grand, intrinsic art.

The breeze moves softly, tree to tree,
It sways in rhythm, wild and free,
And to this dance of life it lends,
A song that never truly ends.

Mirage Among the Branches

Between the branches, fleeting sights,
Of mirrored dreams in filtered light,
Illusions twist with every breeze,
In mystic dances through the trees.

A whisper from the ancient bark,
Glimpsed visions in the forest dark,
Phantom shapes that come and go,
In twilight's gentle ebb and flow.

Reflections in the dew-kissed morn,
Of fears and hopes together born,
A fleeting glance, a shadowed shape,
That from the mind does softly escape.

In the shimmer, secrets hide,
Within the grove, where worlds collide,
A mirage of the past foretold,
In the branches' mystic hold.

Elusive forms in mystic dance,
Through the leaves, in shadowed trance,
The forest holds its mirrored dreams,
In twilight's soft, ethereal beams.

Gliding on Midnight Breezes

Silence whispers through the night,
Stars illuminate with gentle light.
Owl's gaze, alert and wise,
Moon's soft glow in inky skies.

Tree shadows dance in hushed refrain,
Wind sings softly, a ghostly chain.
Nightingale's song, sweet reprise,
Heartbeats sync with midnight's sighs.

Crickets chirp in fields of dew,
Dreams take flight, spirits renew.
Echoed whispers, secrets spoken,
Magic in the dark, unbroken.

Leaves rustle with ancient tales,
Soul and night in harmony sails.
As dawn peeks o'er horizon's crest,
Night's embrace drifts off to rest.

Verdant Voyagers

In valleys deep, where flowers bloom,
Nature's hand dispels the gloom.
Fern and moss, in verdant hue,
Craft a world, vibrant and true.

Through forests dense with emerald light,
Whispered winds guide birds in flight.
Roots entwine in earth's embrace,
Life's pulse found in every place.

Meadows stretch to meet the sky,
Bees hum gentle lullabies.
Petals soft as morning's kiss,
Hills in dew-soaked tenderness.

Streams meander through ancient stones,
Laughter in their jubilant tones.
Carrying tales of time and space,
As nature's verdant voyagers race.

Jungle's Secret Artistry

Vines cascade, a leafy veil,
Through life's green cathedral trail.
Parrots paint with vibrant quill,
Echoes of their voices fill.

Sunlight pierces canopy's shroud,
Nature's voice both soft and loud.
Frogs in symphony announce,
Rhythms in the dusk they pounce.

Butterflies in colors vast,
Wings that whisper of the past.
Each flutter writes a silent song,
Where jungle spirits all belong.

Tiger's gaze, a golden crown,
In shadows where the light's cast down.
Footsteps soft on moss-lined art,
Jungle beats with mystic heart.

Zeniths of Madagascar

Island whispers, ancient lore,
Lemurs leap and spirits soar.
Baobabs against the sky,
Rooted deep, yet reaching high.

Chameleons in camouflage,
Color's shift, a mystic collage.
From rainforests to desert span,
Magic reigns in this wild land.

Rivers wind through fertile fields,
Life in lush abundance yields.
Unique as every leaf and dew,
Madagascar's soul shines true.

Mountains rise with peaks so proud,
Whispers caught in every cloud.
A land of dreams, both near and far,
Guard the realms of Madagascar.

Shadowed Climber

Beneath the moon's pale, silver veil,
A climber dares to scale the night.
With every grip and every tale,
He reaches for the stars so bright.

Mountains whisper secrets low,
Their echoes fade in twilight's grip.
In shadows deep where phantoms flow,
He clings to hope with fingertips.

Through craggy peaks and narrow ledge,
His heart beats steady, strong and true.
The mountain's edge, a sacred pledge,
To conquer dreams and morning dew.

Above the clouds where eagles soar,
He breathes the sky, so pure, so free.
To heights unknown and ever more,
He climbs with soul and destiny.

As dawn ignites the sleeping earth,
He stands where shadows dare to creep,
Embracing light, reborn with worth,
A shadowed climber in the deep.

Graceful Voyager

Upon the waves, a vessel glides,
A voyager with sails unfurled.
Chasing sunsets, ocean tides,
To distant lands and dreams uncurled.

Her compass points to stars above,
Guided by the moonlit night.
With every breath, she whispers love,
To waters deep and skies so bright.

Through tempest strong and silent seas,
She journeys on with heart and grace.
A dance with fate, a wistful breeze,
An endless quest to find her place.

Islands drift in morning's hue,
Harbors call with open arms.
Each new dawn brings visions new,
Shores that sing with hidden charms.

In whispered winds and ocean's song,
Her soul finds peace, her spirit free.
A graceful voyager, brave and strong,
Eternal friend to wind and sea.

Jungle Waltz

In emerald heart where shadows play,
A symphony of life awakes.
The jungle waltz, both wild and gay,
In nature's arms, each dancer takes.

Leaves whisper secrets to the breeze,
Vines entwine in passion's grip.
The chorus of the ancient trees,
With every sway and gentle dip.

Birds of color, vibrant flight,
Weave patterns through the dappled sun.
Their songs ignite the morning light,
A joyous dance, a race begun.

Creatures whisper, soft and low,
In rhythm with the pulsing earth.
To melodies that ebb and flow,
The jungle hums its ancient mirth.

As night descends with velvet grace,
Stars peek through the canopy.
The jungle waltz, in wild embrace,
A timeless dance, forever free.

Branches' Embrace

Amidst the forest, deep and wide,
Where whispered winds weave through the trees,
Beneath the branches, side by side,
The earth and sky share tender ease.

With every breeze, the leaves do sigh,
A gentle caress from nature's hand.
In branches' embrace, dreams can fly,
To worlds beyond our mortal land.

The sunlight filters through the green,
Casting shadows, dappled light.
In this cathedral, pure and serene,
Each branch a guardian in the night.

Birds find solace, nests built high,
Their songs join in the forest hymn.
In branches' arms, they touch the sky,
A symphony on nature's whim.

And when the nightfall softly spreads,
The stars above, like lanterns bright.
In branches' embrace, we lay our heads,
Cradled in the forest's might.

From Dawn to Dusk's Canopy

In rosé blush, the morn alights,
Shadows flee from tender sights,
Whispers of a world anew,
Bid the night its soft adieu.

Golden beams through emerald leaves,
Canvas painted as day weaves,
Birdsong lilts through sapphire skies,
Nature's symphony arise.

Hours stretch with amber grace,
Life's grand theatre in place,
Scenes unfold, a sunlit glow,
In this dance, the world does flow.

Twilight winks with purple hues,
Stars in line, like diamond cues,
Softly fades the day's decree,
To dusk's cosmic canopy.

Nightfall's cloak in velvet spun,
Promises the night begun,
Cycles blend harmoniously,
From dawn to dusk's reverie.

Heights of Midnight Mischief

Midnight cloaks in silver shrouds,
Whispers thick as shadowed clouds,
Elfin spirits laugh and chase,
In the moonlight's soft embrace.

Stars puncture the sky with glee,
Eyes that twinkle mischievously,
Winds that carry secrets aloft,
In their tales, our dreams are brought.

Owls' hoots create a beat,
Rhythms in the darkened street,
Footsteps light on dew-kissed leaves,
Mind and night beguile, deceive.

Mystery in every sigh,
Underneath the watching sky,
Midnight climbs in whispered tones,
Claiming realms of dark unknowns.

Through the veil where shadows creep,
Silent plans in darkness steep,
Woven tricks in moonlight bright,
Heights of mischief, zenith night.

Forest Crests and Crescendos

Morning dew on petals bloom,
Sunrise washes night's perfume,
Birds in choir, day's foretell,
In this glen where spirits dwell.

Treetops etched against the sky,
Timber fingers reaching high,
Canopies in verdant draws,
Bow and sway in nature's laws.

Rivers hum with soothing flow,
Through the valleys, soft and low,
Pebbles sing their water tale,
Crescendos in the forest trail.

Beasts in silence journey forth,
Mark their path by star and north,
Journeys long in shadowed peace,
Forests' whispers never cease.

Sundown flirts with crimson haze,
Night ascends in starry maze,
Forest crests embrace the night,
Nature's hush in fading light.

Murmurs in the Midnight

Midnight cloaks the world so tight,
Candles flicker, casting light,
In the quiet, shadows play,
Murmurs in the night's array.

Soft winds write a whispered prose,
On the leaves where secrets doze,
Silent stars in constellations,
Mark the night's sublime foundations.

Crescent moon, a lustrous arc,
Guides the footsteps through the dark,
Chill of night, a ghostly touch,
Ancient tales that speak so much.

Echoes found where silence dwells,
Woven dreams in midnight spells,
Crickets' song in symphony,
Hum the timeless night's decree.

As the hours drift and weave,
Midnight murmurs softly leave,
Morning comes to kiss the dawn,
Silent whispers, all but gone.

Green Veil Ballet

In forests deep with emerald hue,
A dance begins beneath the blue,
Leaves whisper tales from roots to sky,
As shadows with the sunbeam fly.

A breeze will part the greenish shroud,
Where sunlight's rays are felt and proud,
Nature's stage in perfect play,
A ballet in the light of day.

Twisting, twirling in the air,
Each movement made with utmost care,
The trees and grass join in the fray,
In this grand Green Veil Ballet.

Among the branches, high and free,
A robin sings its melody,
Echoes through the forest vale,
As dancers weave their timeless tale.

Beneath this canopy so vast,
Moments flee yet memories last,
Captured in this fleeting scene,
The forest's dance, forever green.

Nighttime Whispers

When twilight falls, the night begins,
The world of day in shadows dims,
Stars appear in velvet skies,
And whisper secrets as they rise.

The moon hangs low, a silver arc,
Guiding dreams within the dark,
Soft whispers brush the sleeping land,
As lunar beams caress the sand.

In silent glades, the owls take flight,
Their calls dissolve into the night,
Each whisper echoes through the air,
In night's embrace, all burdens bare.

The crickets sing their soft refrain,
A lullaby that soothes the plain,
Beneath the watch of silent eyes,
The whispers of the night arise.

Till dawn arrives with golden seams,
To weave anew our daily dreams,
Remember not the night's soft call,
For whispers fade, remembered all.

Zenith of Silence

Upon the peak where silence reigns,
Above the clouds, beyond the plains,
The world below, a distant stage,
Unheard the cries, unleashed the cage.

The wind is but a whispered pledge,
To sweep the stones and kiss the edge,
Solitude in vast expanse,
A dance unseen, a still romance.

The sky, an azure silent dome,
Embracing all, in spirit roam,
Here thought and breath are found as one,
Beneath the watch of timeless sun.

Each heartbeat felt, each moment pure,
In silence vast, intent secure,
Upon this zenith calm and wise,
Where echoes soar and rise, and rise.

A peace profound, a quiet ode,
In silence found, our hearts exposed,
To reach the zenith, soul and mind,
A silence vast, and so refined.

Dusk's Dancer

As daylight fades in twilight hues,
A silhouette begins its cues,
The stage is set with evening skies,
Where shadows stretch, and day's end lies.

The breeze will guide each gentle step,
In rhythms soft, in moments kept,
A dance of dusk, so light and free,
Performed for stars and moon to see.

Each motion flows with graceful ease,
Among the whispers of the trees,
The world is hushed in golden glow,
As dusk's dancer begins to show.

Reflections caught in dewdrop's might,
Sparkle in the dimming light,
With every turn, with every sway,
Night encroaches, ends the day.

In twilight's arms, the dance concludes,
A final bow in night's soft hues,
Till dawn appears with morning stance,
Thus ends the dusk's enchanting dance.

Forest's Whispered Rhythm

Through ancient trees, the whispers soar,
In tales of myth and days of yore,
Leaves rustle softly, secrets thrive,
In quiet woods, the legends strive.

The moonlight dances on the stream,
A silver thread in nature's seam,
Casting shadows, fleeting, thin,
In the forest, they begin.

Moss-clad roots and ferny fells,
Echo soft with woodland spells,
Winds weave stories through the pines,
In their song, the forest shines.

The forest floor, a tapestry,
Of life's own grand complexity,
With each small creature, life persists,
Within this whispered, timeless mist.

In twilight's gentle, golden gleam,
The forest breathes, a living dream,
With every rustle, chirp, and sigh,
Nature's music fills the sky.

Twilight's Agile Ambassadors

In dusk's embrace, the bats take flight,
Silent shadows in the night,
Through indigo and velvet air,
They paint the sky with practiced care.

With wings like whispers, swift and sleek,
They sail the twilight, mild and meek,
Guided by an unseen thread,
Between the stars, o'er paths they tread.

Their eyes are keen, their purpose clear,
Each night they roam, devoid of fear,
Slicing through the cooling breeze,
Masters of the twilight seas.

As day bids earth a fond adieu,
These dusk emissaries ensue,
Bringing life with every glide,
In night's soft cloak, they do reside.

Ephemeral in their silent trance,
They lead the night in graceful dance,
In moon's soft glow and evening's hue,
Twilight's realm, they nimbly slew.

Secrets Beyond the Canopy

Beneath the emerald, leafy shade,
Where sunlight's tendrils softly fade,
Lie secrets whispered, buried deep,
In the forest, where shadows creep.

The stories of an age-old time,
Softly sung in nature's rhyme,
Hidden paths and ancient lore,
Guarded by the forest floor.

Silken webs that glisten bright,
In the early morning light,
Hold tales of life within their strands,
Spun by nimble woodland hands.

Among the branches, whispers fly,
Told by creatures passing by,
Each a part of nature's weave,
In the canopy, secrets cleave.

Vines entwined in cryptic dance,
Silent secrets left to chance,
Echoes of a world unseen,
Guardians of the forest green.

Twilight's Silent Swing

In twilight's gentle, quiet swing,
The forest breathes as nightbirds sing,
A lullaby from dusk 'til dawn,
As night and day, in rhythm, yawn.

Softly, gently, shadows fall,
Covering earth in a velvet shawl,
The silent wing of owls in flight,
Marks the start of twilight's night.

Stars emerge in quiet gleam,
Awakening the nighttime dream,
With every glance, a story told,
In twilight's arms, the night's unfold.

The forest hums a silent tune,
Beneath the watchful, rising moon,
With every step, the creatures tread,
Where day has vanished, night has spread.

Within the hush, beneath the sky,
Twilight whispers, spirits lie,
In every sway of leaf and bough,
Twilight sings its silent vow.

Milton Keynes UK
Ingram Content Group UK Ltd.
UKHW022239280824
447491UK00010B/282

9 789916 864548